Internet Predators

By Toney Allman

ERICKSON PRESS
Yankton, South Dakota

ERICKSON PRESS

For more information, contact
Erickson Press
329 Broadway
PO Box 33
Yankton, SD 57078

Or you can visit our internet site at www.ericksonpress.com

Library of Congress Control Number: 200693815
ISBN-10: 1-60217-000-2
ISBN-13: 978-1-60217-000-1

Printed in the United States of America

Contents

Introduction: Plague of the Internet   4

Chapter 1: Cyber-Creeps   7

Chapter 2: Survivors   19

Chapter 3: Catching Predators   32

Chapter 4: Staying Safe   45

Notes   56

Glossary   59

Bibliography   60

Index   62

Picture Credits   64

About the Author   64

Plague of the Internet

The Internet has changed people's lives around the world. People use email. They send instant messages. They post on blogs. They go to chat rooms. They meet new people. They learn new things. Yet rotten things can happen on the Internet. Sex predators use the Internet, too. They talk to each other. They share tactics. They trade pictures of pornography, or porn. And they try to find children and teens to talk to and meet. Sadly, finding young victims is easy. Almost 1 billion people use the Internet. At least 24 million are children and teens.

Most young people never meet an Internet predator. But some do. Some victims fall in love. They may run away to meet the predator in person. A few never come home. Others agree to meet strangers from the Internet and are molested or raped. Some are talked into performing sex acts at the computer. Others share photos of themselves. And these end up on sexy Web sites. Many people see them.

On television, NBC has a show about predators. It is part of NBC's *Dateline* series. It is called "To Catch a Predator." The series says Internet sex predators are everywhere. Not everyone agrees that it is that bad, but predators are a problem. Young people are hurt because predators pretend to care about them. Young people tend to trust adults they meet on the Internet. But the predators are just

Rick Woody holds up a picture of his daughter Kacie. She was kidnapped and killed by a man she met in a chat room.

Victims on the Internet

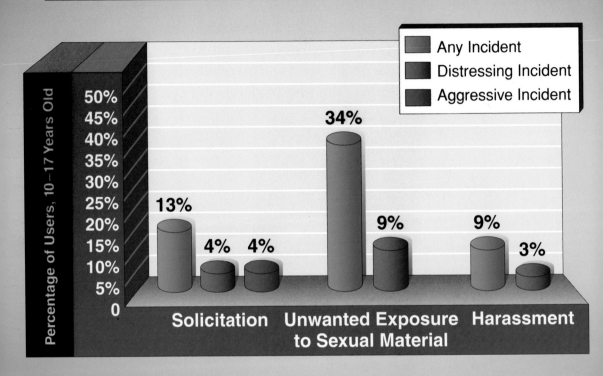

Legend:
- Any Incident
- Distressing Incident
- Aggressive Incident

Percentage of Users, 10–17 Years Old

50%
45%
40%
35%
30%
25%
20%
15%
10%
5%
0

Solicitation — 13%, 4%, 4%

Unwanted Exposure to Sexual Material — 34%, 9%

Harassment — 9%, 3%

Source: National Center for Missing and Exploited Children, 2006.

tricking them. Predators do not love their victims. They use them. No one deserves to be conned that way.

Internet predators scare lawmakers. They worry police. They upset parents. Many experts think young people can fix the problem. Young people have to learn about Internet predators. That is what will keep them safe.

Chapter 1

Cyber-Creeps

Before the Internet, Toby Studabaker might have been slinking through a mall. He might have sat in his car outside a school. He might have lurked on neighborhood streets. But he was not in any of these places in 2003. He was on a Web site for kids called NeoPets.com. There he met a girl in England. She was 11 years old. Studabaker lived in Michigan. He made friends with the girl online. It was not a healthy friendship. Studabaker was 32 years old and an Internet predator.

Pedophiles

Internet predators are pedophiles. More than 95 percent of them are men. They want to use children and teens for sex. They may also be people who collect porn. Sometimes they are looking for people to hurt. Predators are not common on the Internet. Only about 1 young person out of every

Toby Studabaker was a U.S. marine who served in Afghanistan. Here he makes a call on his cell phone.

33 meets a predator online. That is 725,000 out of 24 million. Still, dangerous predators are on the Internet. Many are in chat rooms. Some experts believe that the Internet has made it easier for pedophiles to find kids. In 2005 the U.S. Department of Justice said that 13 percent of young people online got a message asking for sex talk or sex. This is called solicitation. That is about 3.2 million people between the ages of ten

and seventeen. About 3 percent of these messages are from Internet predators. Studabaker was one of those predators. He was a pedophile who found a victim.

Studabaker spent a lot of time emailing with his new young friend. He was interested in everything she had to say. He cared about her ideas and problems. He had a way to make his young victim love and trust him. It is called grooming.

Grooming the Victim

Grooming is the way predators make a bond of deep trust between themselves and their victims. It starts with simple questions. Studabaker asked his victim what she liked to do. He asked about her hobbies, her schoolwork, and her friends. He listened to her problems. His replies were always sweet and kind. He said he liked and disliked the same things she did. He was very patient. Then he started talking about love and sex. He told the girl that all sex talk and behavior between them were normal. After many months, he made himself the girl's best friend. He told her he loved her. Sometimes the two spent eleven hours a day on the Internet, chatting and emailing. The young girl had a webcam. Studabaker got the girl to let him watch her undress. He showered her with compliments. He told her how beautiful she was. He said he never loved anyone so much.

Studabaker's grooming worked. His victim came to love and trust him completely. When she was twelve, Studabaker said he wanted to fly to England to visit her. He wrote that he could not bear to be apart from her anymore. He said he wanted to spend his whole life with her. Studabaker also told her, "You are the one: my soulmate. I would [not] change a thing about you. I feel in love with you as you are, and I never want to change that."[1] His victim believed everything he wrote. She believed his promise that their age difference did not matter. She believed they had true love together. At his urging, she kept their love secret from her parents. She and Studabaker made plans to run away together.

Studabaker was a success as a predator because he got his victim to love him. He and his young victim did run away together. They spent four days hiding in France. The girl's scared parents went to the police. They reported her missing. The police searched for the missing girl. The story was on TV. Studabaker got nervous. He

Tactics

Most Internet predators use grooming. They do not use force. They do not lie about their age. They want victims to have sex willingly. Only about 16 percent of predators use force. Only about 5 percent pretend to be teens.

A police van carries Toby Studabaker to trial in an English court.

put the girl on a plane and sent her home. He tried to run away to Germany. He was arrested before he made it. After a trial, he was sent to prison in England for having sex with a child.

His True Colors

As police learned more about Studabaker, it was clear that his young victim was not his soulmate. She was not the love of his life. He had already been accused of molesting kids. He had child porn stored on his computer. The girl was just someone to use for sex.

These facts were not known to most people who knew Studabaker. Friends and neighbors knew a different side of him. They knew he went to church. They knew he had spent a year in Bible college. They knew he had been married. They knew he was a marine who had served bravely in Afghanistan. They did not know about his secret life. They did not know he was an Internet predator.

Toby Studabaker was sent to prison in England for having sex with an underage girl.

Love Lies

Such a secret life is common among pedophiles. Julian Morrel was a doctor in London. He was 42 years old. He was also a pedophile. In 2004 he lured a 14-year-old girl over the Internet. He registered at a chat room called Pre-Teen Chat. He wanted to meet young victims. Unlike Studabaker, Morrel hid his age. He pretended to be 15 years old. Soon he met a 14-year-old Welsh girl online. He spent a month emailing her. He sent her lots of text messages. Morrel groomed the girl. He gained her trust. Then she agreed to meet him. She went to a campground near her home.

Morrel drove there from London. He brought a tent with him.

The two met in person. It was clear at once that Morrel was not 15. He still hid his real age of 42. He told the girl he was 32. He had sex with her. Secret meetings between the two went on for about a month. Then the girl's parents found out. Morrel was arrested. His victim felt very sad. She had believed Morrel loved her. She was upset and

Grooming Tricks

Predators have tricky ways to make people want to be with them. A predator may lurk in chat rooms. He may read profiles. He finds out all about a young person before he sends a message. This is how he knows what that person likes and wants. Then he sends nice, friendly messages. Once he makes friends, he gives lots of compliments. He uses nicknames like "sweetie" or "pumpkin." He pretends to be very understanding. He may be careful not to talk about sex. Then he disappears from the Internet for a few days. This trick makes the victim worry and miss his or her new friend. When the predator returns, the victim is relieved. He or she now has feelings for the predator. The predator uses love as bait to draw in the victim. But the love is not real. Often, a predator is grooming several young people at the same time. Each one feels special but no one is. All of them are just sex objects to the predator.

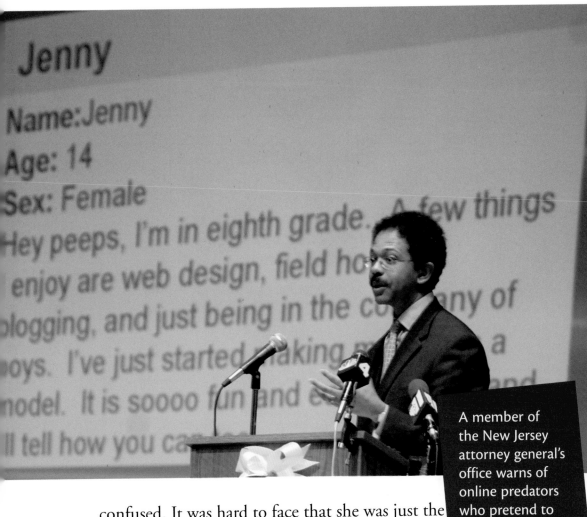

A member of
the New Jersey
attorney general's
office warns of
online predators
who pretend to
be teens.

confused. It was hard to face that she was just the
victim of a predator. The police found out that
Morrel collected child porn. He was seeking child
sex, not love.

Danger

Being tricked and used is terrible and painful. But
some Internet predators do even more damage. A

few Internet predators get what they want by force. They are very cruel. They start off like other predators. They use grooming and talk of love. But when a meeting takes place, this kind of predator hurts his victim.

Alicia Kozakiewicz was 13 years old when she was tricked by Scott Tyree. He was 38 years old. Alicia lived near Pittsburgh, Pennsylvania. Tyree lived in Herndon, Virginia. On the Internet, Tyree flattered Alicia. He was kind and nice. Alicia thought Tyree was a good friend. Tyree groomed Alicia for a month. She had no idea

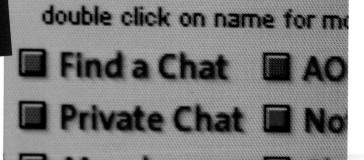

23 people here

Holly 18f Girl
Sxkaliber
FTLKelly
CRA1G 1103
Biglefty2
Easy Teen Girl

double click on name for mo

Find a Chat   AO

Private Chat   No

The screen name "Easy Teen Girl" is a bad idea. It may attract online predators.

It Is a Sickness

Cris Italia is a reporter. He works for the Herald Community Newspapers in New York. He talked to a predator called Scott in January 2004. Scott told Italia that he is a pedophile. He said it is a sickness. Scott was in prison. He had sex with a girl he met online. She was only twelve years old. Scott no longer owns a computer. If he did, he knows he would look for porn. He would try to meet young girls. He is in counseling now. He is trying to change. Scott told Italia, "I get urges all the time. . . . I hope I can reduce the urges, but sometimes it's uncontrollable."

Quoted in Cris Italia, "Mind of a Pedophile: Convicted Child Abuser Admits Sickness," (NewYork) Herald Community Newspapers, Zwire, January 22, 2004. (www.zwire.com/site/news.cfm?newsid=10849893& BRD=1601&PAG= 461&dept_i).

that Tyree wanted a "sex slave."[2] He told online friends that he was going to find a victim.

Alicia agreed to meet Tyree one night in January 2002. Tyree drove Alicia to his apartment. He kept her there. Then he sent a message to an online buddy. He bragged, "I got one."[3] He posted a webcam picture to prove it. Tyree's buddy was scared by what he saw. He tipped off police and the Federal Bureau of Investigation (FBI). They searched for Alicia for four days. Then they found Tyree's address in Virginia. They broke into his home. There they found Alicia chained in a bedroom. She had a collar around her neck. She was terrified and beaten, but she was alive. Her biggest challenge would be to find a way to get over what had happened.

Tyree was arrested and sent to prison. He was like many other predators. He seemed normal. No one had guessed what he was really like. He had been married and divorced. He had a daughter who was twelve years old. He worked as a computer programmer. He seemed like everyone else.

Not Ordinary at All

Millions of people use the Internet every day. Most of them are okay. Yet predators are there. One study found out that 50,000 sex predators are online every hour. But it is hard to know who they are. Steve Whitley is a police officer in North Carolina. He says most predators seem to be "just a guy like you and me. They look like ordinary people, and it's scary."[4]

Predators, though, are not normal people. They are attracted to children and teens. They seek out victims and do lasting damage. The young people who are caught in the predators' traps are the ones who pay in the end.

Chapter 2

Survivors

At seventeen, Alicia Kozakiewicz is doing well. She is not a victim now. She is a survivor. She got over what Tyree did to her. Today, Alicia gives talks to other young people. She warns them about predators. She explains how people can be fooled by strangers. In many ways, Alicia is a good example of a person who falls for a predator.

Who Is at Risk?

Experts used to believe that only shy loners were fooled by sex predators. They thought only misfits got tricked. They thought happy teens were not fooled by grooming. Other experts said that angry teens were the ones who took the risks. These rebels liked the thrill of meeting up with strangers. None of this is so. Some victims of pedophiles may be loners. Some may be rebels. But most are just normal people who let down their guard.

Alicia, for example, had loving parents. She had many friends. She was an honor-roll student. She seemed happy at home and in school. But anyone can have problems. Anyone can be unhappy once in a while. Everyone is worried or confused sometimes.

People who fall prey to pedophiles may just be feeling a little sad or lonely. They could be unsure about themselves. They may be curious about sex. They may want to explore and learn about new people. Some of them just may be very kind people. They may be eager to help a stranger who wants a friend. Internet predators are very, very

Forced to Give In

Bobbi Davis was 14 years old. She lived in Arizona. She met a man named Al in a chat room. She thought he was a friend. She told him her phone number. Bobbi and Al emailed and talked every day. When Al asked to meet her, Bobbi agreed. He took her to a hotel room. Bobbi did not want to have sex. Al raped her. Then he let Bobbi go home. She was afraid to tell anyone what had happened. She kept it a secret for two years. Finally, she told her story. The man was sent to prison. Bobbi is grown now but she cannot forget the rape. She still has nightmares. Bobbi is a survivor but she is very angry about the hurt that sex predators cause.

good at taking advantage of people. They are great liars and con artists. Their victims may suffer for a long time.

Katie's Story

Katie Tarbox was a popular thirteen-year-old who lived in Connecticut. She was an athlete. She was a member of her school's swim team. She found out about America Online (AOL) chat rooms in 1995, when the Internet was fairly new. Katie was at an unhappy time in her life. Her parents were busy with work. They did not have time to talk with her. Katie's friends were starting to date. She did not feel ready. She was not sure of herself. She worried about her looks. She wondered about her future. Katie did not know it but she was ripe for a predator's tricks.

Katie knew all about the creeps and liars who could be online. But Mark from California seemed different. He and Katie met in an AOL chat room. Mark was 23 years old but he had time to talk. He was interesting and smart. He offered friendship. He told Katie that their age difference did not matter. He wrote to her, "In other countries no one would even care. . . . I am not concerned about it, so you shouldn't be either."[5] In their first

Smarter now about Internet dangers, Katie Tarbox logs onto her Internet account at home.

chat, Mark asked Katie for her phone number. Soon the two were talking all the time. They chatted online. They talked on the phone. For Katie, being friends with Mark was wonderful and important. Mark seemed very special.

Mark begged to meet Katie in person. Finally after six months of talking, Katie agreed. She would meet Mark while she was at a swim-team event in Texas. The girls on the team stayed in a Texas hotel. Mark got a room there too. Katie sneaked up to Mark's room. Almost at once, Mark wanted sex. He kissed and touched Katie. Then came a knock at the door. The team chaperones and Katie's mother burst into the room. They exploded in anger.

The Aftermath

Katie's Internet friendship was over. Her mother called the police. Soon Katie had to face some hard facts. The predator's name was not Mark. He was Frank Kufrovich. He was not 23. He was 41. The FBI became involved in the case. From the FBI, Katie learned that Frank was a pedophile. He had used other girls and boys. He had child porn on his computer. Katie was just another victim.

It took two years to bring Kufrovich to trial for molesting Katie. Later, she said:

Gradually, the man who had been my friend, who had listened to me and cared for me so deeply, was fading from view. He was being replaced by the image of a porn-obsessed child molester named Frank Kufrovich. This was not my Mark. But he was the one who had created Mark. He only existed in my heart, and he was dying.[6]

Katie had to deal with the truth about Kufrovich. She had to go to court. It upset her very much. She began to have emotional problems. She slept and ate poorly. She often vomited. She could not do her work in school. She believed she was the bad one. She says, "I knew he was older than

Katie Tarbox sits on her mother's lap with her family around her. Their support helped her to recover.

Katie Tarbox wrote a book about her ordeal. It also helped her to heal.

me—everyone said that was why he was being punished—but I still felt responsible."[7]

Katie's life could have been ruined by Kufrovich's lies. She did not let that happen. At age sixteen, she got counseling. She learned not to blame herself. When she was eighteen, she wrote a book about what had happened to her. She used her terrible journey to help and warn others. She turned herself from a victim into a survivor. She explains, "Life is not about setbacks, but how you overcome them."[8]

Paying a Huge Price

Katie got over her experience with a sex predator. Some people do not. A few vanish and are never seen again. Christina Long was one of the unlucky ones. She was killed in 2002 when she was 13 years old. Christina lived in Connecticut. She was popular in school. She was an A student. She was a cheerleader. Christina also had a secret life. She was curious about sex. She wanted excitement. She

Saul Dos Reis (above) appears in court. He admitted to killing Christina Long. Members of his family look upset as they leave the courthouse (inset).

took risks. She agreed to have sex with someone she met on MySpace. His name was Saul Dos Reis. He was 25 years old. He killed Christina when he met her. It was the first known murder by an Internet predator in the United States. Such awful killings are rare. Fewer than 5 percent of meetings with Internet predators turn violent. But with strangers, no one can be sure what will happen.

Justin's Story

Girls are not the only ones targeted by Internet predators. In 2000 Justin Berry was thirteen years old. He lived in California. He had his own Web site and a webcam. He says, "I hoped the webcam

Justin Berry speaks to senators about Internet child porn and other dangers.

Criminal Teens

Not all dangerous people on the Internet are adults. In Chicago in 2006, three young men raped a teen girl they met on MySpace. They were seventeen, eighteen, and fifteen. The girl went willingly to the home of one of her new "friends." There, the four drank alcohol and played video games. But the girl passed out. The young men raped her. When they were done, they dumped her in an alley. Finally, she was able to get back home.

would help me meet other teenagers online, maybe even find a few girls my age."[9] Justin did not meet any teens. He met adult men. They were friendly and kind. They sent him gifts through an Amazon.com wish list. Then one of his new friends asked Justin to take off his shirt for the webcam. He said he would pay Justin $50 with a PayPal account. It seemed easy. Justin wanted the money. So he did it. That began an awful way of life. Justin got into Internet porn and cybersex.

Many men visited Justin's Web site. They showered him with attention. They offered him money and gifts to show more and more. Justin slowly gave in. These people were his friends. He says, "They complimented me all the time. They told me I was smart, they told me I was handsome."[10] Then the predators asked to meet him.

Justin agreed, and he was molested. At last, Justin did not care what happened to him. He would do anything for the camera. He would do anything for the men who had become his customers. His pictures were shared all over the Internet. He had sex for the camera. Sometimes he was alone and sometimes with others.

Escape

By 2005, when he was eighteen, Justin felt his life had fallen apart. He did not understand how he had gotten in so deeply. He wanted to get away. He wanted to die. He thought of himself as "a piece of meat, for sale to the highest bidder."[11]

A *New York Times* reporter contacted Justin online. Justin grabbed the chance to change. He told the reporter his story. He decided to shut down his Web site and fight online porn. Today, Justin has turned his life around. He returned to school. He started going to church. He got counseling. In 2006 he spoke before Congress about Internet predators. He described the teens who are sucked into the cybersex world. He says, "I didn't want these people to hurt any more kids. I didn't want anyone else to live the life I lived."[12]

It Has to Stop

Almost all victims of Internet predators suffer in the end. The lucky ones survive. But it has become clear that something must be done to stop predators.

Chapter 3

Catching Predators

People today take Internet predators very seriously. They want to stop the predators. They want to catch predators who are looking for victims. The easiest way to fight sex predators is with stings.

In an Internet sting, police or someone working with police goes undercover. He or she becomes a decoy. The decoy signs into a chat room. Then the decoy pretends to be a kid. The decoy waits to be contacted. If a predator starts to chat, the decoy answers in a friendly way. If the predator asks for a meeting, one is set up. The predator goes to the meeting place. He expects to meet a kid. Instead, the predator is arrested.

Laws about sex between adults and teens are not the same in all states. In some states, the legal age may be 18. In others, it may be 16. It depends on what the predator tries to do. The decoys often say they are 13 or 14. Some stings are set up in rented houses. Others happen in public places, like parks. Stings work almost any-

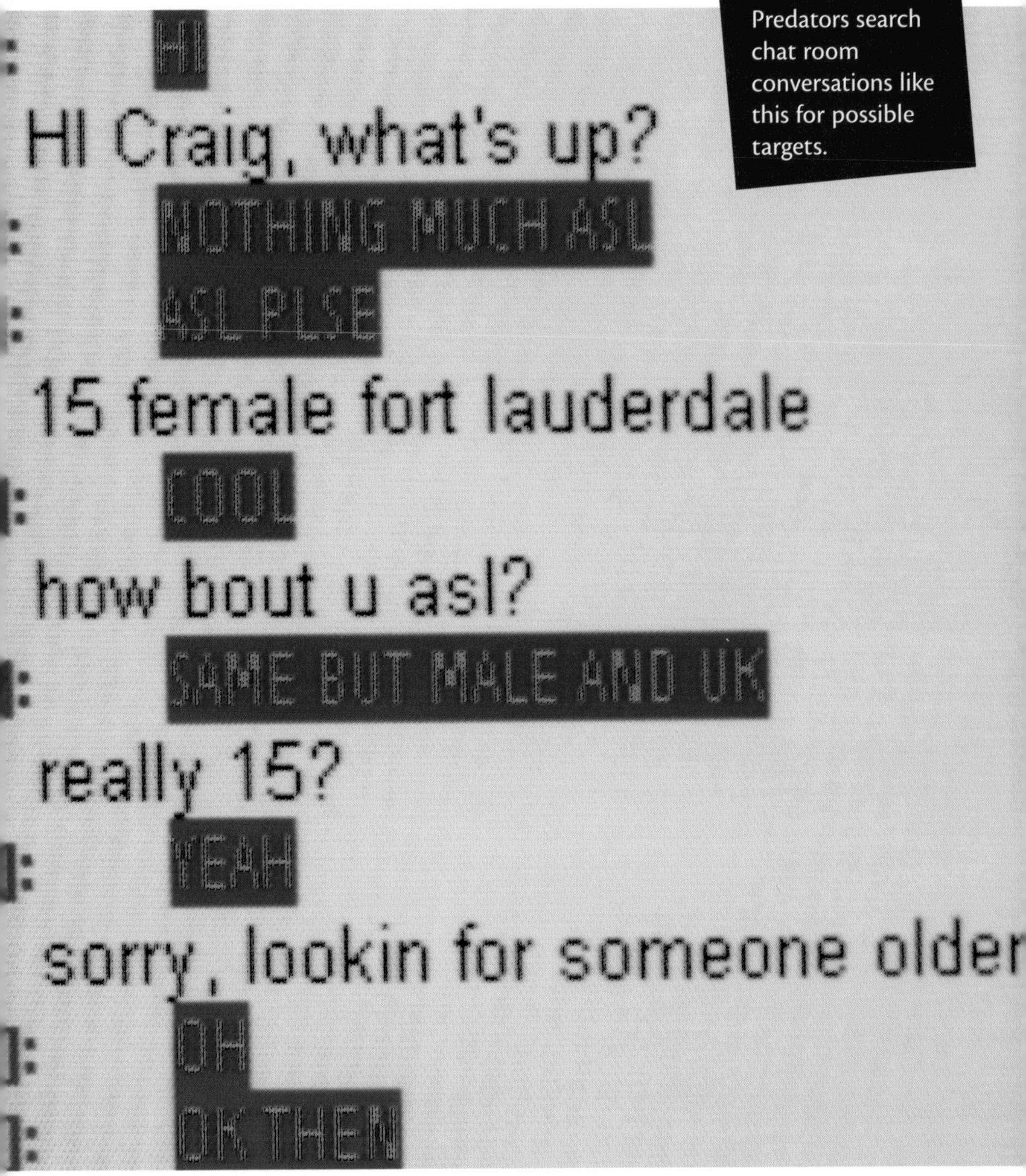

HI

HI Craig, what's up?

NOTHING MUCH ASL

ASL PLSE

15 female fort lauderdale

COOL

how bout u asl?

SAME BUT MALE AND UK

really 15?

YEAH

sorry, lookin for someone older

OH

OK THEN

In 2003 Tom Ridge (left), head of Homeland Security, and John Walsh (right), host of *America's Most Wanted*, speak to reporters about fighting pedophiles.

where in the United States. Reporter Mark Vasto says, "This is mainly because the problem, namely the sexual predator, can be found in [almost] every community."[13]

A Sting in Missouri

In 2006 police in one Missouri county set up a sting to catch predators. They signed into an Internet chat room. They made up a screen name for a girl named Abbey. They signed her in as abbey_kcmo. They said she was 14 years old. A

35-year-old man began to chat with the decoy. His name was David Jackson. Jackson began to talk about sex after only seven minutes. He asked Abbey to meet him. A meeting was set up for the next day. Jackson came to the undercover house. He brought alcohol, condoms, and a camera. Jackson did not get what he wanted. He was arrested. In court, Jackson pleaded guilty. He was sent to prison for five years. The prosecutor says, "If this defendant had been talking to a real girl, she would probably have ended up intoxicated [drunk] and raped, while the defendant recorded the whole ordeal on videotape."[14]

The Sting Experts

Stings are a good way to catch Internet predators. Many police departments use them today. Sometimes the police team up with a special group on the Internet. They are members of a Web site called Perverted-Justice.com or PeeJ. PeeJ was set up in 2003. Its goal is to expose Internet predators to the world. PeeJ members know that predators hurt many young people. They hate Internet predators. PeeJ wants to make predators afraid. PeeJ members are trained to pose as children or teens online. They wait for predators to contact them. They keep logs of those chats. They post the chat logs and the predators' real names on their Web site. They want to shame the predators. They tell the world their names. PeeJ is a leader in fighting online sex predators.

The members of PeeJ know how to trick predators. Police officers use their help to set up stings. Mitch Madruga is a detective in Gilroy, California. He worked with PeeJ to catch Jason Bell in 2005. Madruga was already being a decoy on the Internet. He posed as a girl named Catrina. He said she was thirteen years old. Bell sent Catrina nude pictures of himself. He said he wanted to

To catch online sex predators, officer Don Condon pretends to be a young person in a chat room.

A Perverted-Justice Member

Wendy O'Connell lives in Mississippi. She is 25 years old. When she was younger she did not know about Internet predators. Then she found the Perverted-Justice Web site. She learned how predators are everywhere. It made her angry. She had friends who had been abused. She decided to join PeeJ. She became a member in 2003. Today she helps PeeJ work with police to catch predators. Sometimes she spends 70 hours a week at this job. She has a big goal for the future. She wants to be out of a job. She wants predators to be confused. She wants them to be scared. She wants them to worry about who they are talking to when they email a teen. She wants teens to be smart. She does not want any teens to be taken in by a sex predator. She knows that will not happen any time soon. But she hopes her work is getting the Internet closer to her goal.

have sex with her. He told her to wear pantyhose to their meeting. He wanted to use them to tie her up. He said it would be fun.

Now Madruga needed a decoy to talk to Bell on the phone. He asked a PeeJ decoy to do it. The PeeJ decoy talked with Bell. She agreed to meet him that night in a park. Bell came to the park. Madruga was waiting to arrest him. Madruga says PeeJ is a good tool for police to use. He says, "If we can stop something from happening, from someone becoming a victim, then it's worth it."[15]

The members of PeeJ feel the same way. They help police, the FBI, the Secret Service, and TV reporters stop online predators. Del Harvey is one staff member at PeeJ. She is 23 and lives in California. She often spends 80 hours a week working on the PeeJ Web site. She chats in chat rooms. She talks on the phone. Harvey says her hard work is "very, very much worth it to know at the end of the day that you made a difference."[16]

Dateline Undercover

Harvey also works for *Dateline NBC*. Since 2004 *Dateline* has had a show called "To Catch a

Taking it Personally

People join Perverted-Justice for different reasons. About half of the members were molested when they were kids. They want to stop other predators. Not all PeeJ members were victims. Some know people who were abused. Others just think predators are creeps. The group has 65 people on staff. It has more than 40,000 members. The group's goal is to put an end to Internet dangers.

Predator." The show films sex predators. The goal of the show is to scare off predators from real teens. *Dateline* sets up stings. PeeJ members help. They pretend to be teens online. Predators chat with the decoys about sex. PeeJ keeps logs of everything the predators say. *Dateline* rents a house for each show. PeeJ decoys tell the predators that they live there. They say they are home alone. They tell the predator to come and visit. Predators show up for dates with teens. Then TV cameras record the men who show up.

In her role as a decoy, Harvey dresses like a young teen. She is a small woman. She wears a hoodie and baggy pants. She wears a cap to cover her hair. She waits for the predator to arrive. Then she lets him see her from a distance. As he walks in the door, she calls to her visitor from the next room. She promises to join him soon. Instead, *Dateline* reporter Chris Hansen walks in. He exposes the man on national TV. Outside, local police wait to arrest him as he leaves. *Dateline*

How Old?

The CyberCollege (www.cybercollege.com/ index.htm) is an Internet Web site. It has a chart about the ages of Internet predators. It also lists the ages of victims. Seventy-six percent of victims are between 13 and 15. Seventy-six percent of the predators are older than 25.

Ages of Victims

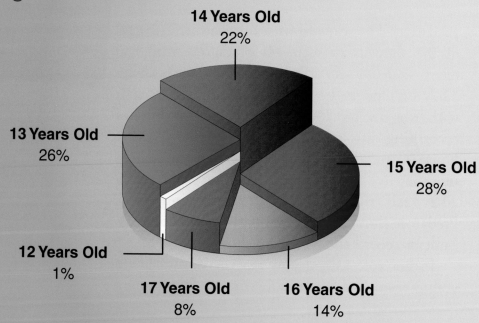

14 Years Old
22%

13 Years Old
26%

15 Years Old
28%

12 Years Old
1%

17 Years Old
8%

16 Years Old
14%

stings have been set up in six different states. They exposed 178 predators between 2004 and 2006.

Caught

Dateline's third show aired in February 2006. It took place in California. *Dateline* rented a house. Hidden cameras were placed inside. Local police

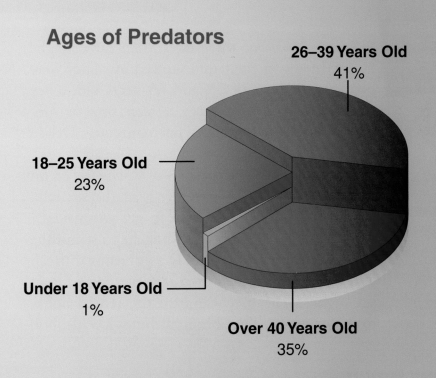

Ages of Predators

26–39 Years Old
41%

18–25 Years Old
23%

Under 18 Years Old
1%

Over 40 Years Old
35%

Tammy Basham sits at her home computer. She discovered that an adult man had made friends with her twelve-year-old daughter online.

hid next door. For three days, men came to the house. In all, 51 predators showed up. They were between the ages of 19 and 65 years old. They thought they would meet a teen boy or girl. Harvey told the predators her name was Del so she could pose as a boy or a girl.

The predators said all sorts of things to Del on the Internet. *Dateline* saved logs of the sex talk. One man said, "Would love to get you naked." Another said, "Hey do you want me to spend the night?" A third said, "You are a gorgeous thirteen year old boy."[17] Several men sent pictures of their sex organs. The men came to the rented house ready for action. They brought things like alcohol, whipped cream, pies, video cameras, condoms, CDs, and Viagra.

Anyone Can Be a Predator

Hansen and his news team were shocked to find so many predators. They came from all walks of life. Many were married. Some had kids of their own. They had many different jobs. One was an actor. One was a construction worker. One was a songwriter. One was a salesman. Another was a teacher. There were also men with criminal records. One had stalked a woman. Another had been found guilty of manslaughter. One man had raped a woman and gone to prison. Another man had been arrested, too. He had had sex with a fifteen-year-old. Another was a known sex offender. Sergeant Chad Bianco was really glad to have caught that one. He says, "They're nice men or nice boys that appear on the Internet, but when they actually show up at your front door or in your living room, then you find out who really was on the other end of that Internet connection."[18]

Making a Difference

Dateline keeps setting up stings. Perverted-Justice sets up stings. Police in many states set up stings.

They all want to catch and scare Internet predators. They hope predators will notice the stings. They hope predators will be too scared to seek out young people. They hope predators will fear arrest. And then they might stop chatting with young people online.

Some predators do worry about stings. But others do not stop trying to meet young people. They know about stings. But they try anyway. Sex predators cannot be stopped by stings alone. They will never truly be stopped until people learn how to protect themselves.

Chapter 4

Staying Safe

Today, many people work to make users safe online. Stings are common. Internet sites try to protect users. New laws have been passed. Teens are smarter about predators too. They are learning about predators' tricks. That is how the predators are really stopped.

Slowing the Sleaze

Crimes Against Children Research Center did a study in 2001. It showed that 20 percent of young people got sex messages from strangers online. That number had dropped to 13 percent by 2005. Stings have helped this happen. New laws have also helped. Web sites police themselves too. A big change is that more and more teens delete sex messages. They do not answer. The online world is getting wise to predators.

The threat of prison also can stop predators. Thirty-six states have new Internet laws. These laws make it a crime to be a sex predator on the

Internet. It is a crime for an adult to ask a young person to have sex. Kim Mercer is a police officer in California. She says, "It is against the law for an adult to talk to a kid about sex online."[19] In some states, a predator can get twenty years in prison. Even the FBI does not know how many Internet predators there are. But it does say that stings and tough laws mean fewer victims.

Age of Consent by State

Heterosexual

Each state has laws that dictate the age a person can legally consent to sex. An adult cannot legally engage in sexual intercourse with persons below the age of consent.

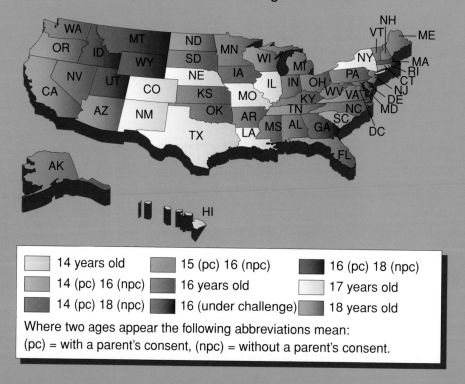

	14 years old		15 (pc) 16 (npc)		16 (pc) 18 (npc)
	14 (pc) 16 (npc)		16 years old		17 years old
	14 (pc) 18 (npc)		16 (under challenge)		18 years old

Where two ages appear the following abbreviations mean:
(pc) = with a parent's consent, (npc) = without a parent's consent.

Policing Web Sites

Internet social sites try to stop visits by predators, too. MySpace is the biggest social site. It has 76 million users. Twenty percent of the users are teens. One-third of the people who work for MySpace are there to police the site. The site also has a list of safety tips for users.

Homosexual

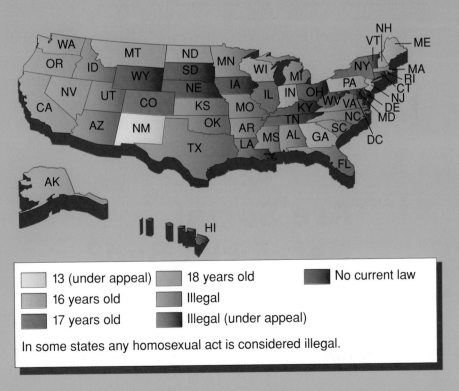

13 (under appeal)	18 years old	No current law
16 years old	Illegal	
17 years old	Illegal (under appeal)	

In some states any homosexual act is considered illegal.

Other Web sites fight predators the same way. They keep a close eye on chat rooms. TeenSpot uses a computer program that watches chats. It catches the common words that sex predators use. Then it reports the message to a staff member. Teens also can report sleazy messages to a 911 room. TeenSpot lists safety tips that warn all its users about predators.

Are Social Networks Bad?

Some people do not think that Web sites do enough. Congress is thinking about a new law.

The law would force schools and libraries to block social Web sites. Young people could not use sites like MySpace in schools or libraries. They could not see profiles. They could not post any profiles. They could not get into discussion boards or chat rooms. They might not even be able to use email. Some experts think this is the only way to protect young people from Internet predators.

Other experts say this law is wrong. It would hurt kids. It does not make sense. It would be like closing shopping malls to save children from strangers. Danah Boyd is a student at the University of California at Berkeley. She is studying how young people use the Internet. She

A woman reads a page on the MySpace Web site. Social networks like MySpace are gathering places for teens.

Teens and Social Sites

Teens enjoy social sites. Experts say that 61 percent have Web pages on sites like MySpace and Xanga. But many teens do not know about online safety. Half of them post real photos on their Web pages. Many reply to strangers who post messages to them. Some will agree to meet strangers in person. About half of all teens think it is safe to meet Internet friends in person. These teens do not know they are in danger. But teens who take classes in Internet safety change their minds. They learn about sex predators. They become aware of how predators look for teens. Then 84 percent of them believe it is not safe to meet Internet friends in person.

thinks social sites are good for young people. There are few places where teens can gather. She says that social sites "give youth a space to hang out. . . ."[20] Boyd's partner in the study is a teacher in a Massachusetts college. He says the Internet should be seen as a training ground for kids. It is teaching the country's future leaders. Both experts believe that young people should be allowed to use social sites. They say that people learn to connect with others on the Internet. They learn social skills in places like MySpace. They say the sites should not be blocked. Kids just need education.

Teaching Safety

I-SAFE is one Web site for Internet education. It has lessons for young people and their parents. They learn about predators. They get tips about how to stay safe on the Internet. Students learn about cybersex and porn. Predators are often into these things. Students learn not to share photos with an online friend. They learn that webcam images can be used by predators. The predator might post private pictures on porn sites. Students also learn never to make a date with anyone they meet online. They learn to ignore sex messages. They learn to delete them and block the sender.

Florida detectives hunt online for sex predators who try to hook up with young people.

Stacey DeLuca patrols the Internet at home. She acts as a decoy for online stings.

Weron2u is a Web site from Canada. It says, "We're too smart for Internet perverts."[21] The site lists many tips for staying safe. The most important tip is "give them nothing."[22] People think nobody knows who they are on the Internet. That is true. But it is important to stay truly unknown. Real names should always be a secret from strangers. It is easy to forget that blogs and social sites are public places. Predators may be in these places looking for clues. They may try to figure out someone's real name. They may try to learn where a teen lives. Weron2u says that people should never post real names or addresses. They should not post photos. They should keep schools, clubs, and phone numbers secret. Even a user-name can give a predator a clue about someone. "Valley-Cheerleader," for example, is a bad user-name choice for a student at Valley High School.

Learning the Predator's Tactics

A Canadian company named LiveWires Design made up a CD-ROM game called Missing. It shows examples of tactics and tricks that predators use. Teens play this game and pretend they are detectives. They must track down a teenage boy who has been lured by a sex predator. The Missing game is based on a true story. It is about a teen who fell for the promises of a predator. Game players learn real things a predator might say. They learn to recognize a predator's tricks. They learn how a predator might act. They know what he might say.

One girl who played this game was named Katie. Katie was fifteen years old when she fell in love with an Internet predator. She thought he was a friend. He sent her presents. He made her happy. Katie wanted to meet her friend in person. But the police learned about the predator. The meeting never took place. Then Katie played the Missing game. The predator in the game used exactly the same lines her "friend" had used with her. Katie understood that she was not special to her "friend." She was the victim of a con man. She says today, "Every child is vulnerable for this, every boy, girl, sitting online is a victim waiting to happen if they're not prepared."[23] The Missing game helps young people to understand grooming. It prepares them to reject fake friendships.

Some sex messages from predators are easy to spot. Most people who receive such messages just delete them. But some predators are tricky. They are patient. They are willing to spend weeks or months grooming their victims. They seem kind and sweet. They flatter their victims. They may send photos of themselves. The pictures may not be real. They may pretend they are teens. They seem so safe that their victims trust them. There is no way to know who is telling the truth on the Internet. People have to get wise to online predators.

MySpace Safety Tips

- **Don't forget that your profile and MySpace forums are public spaces.**
- **People aren't always who they say they are. Be careful adding strangers to your friends list.**
- **Harassment, hate speech, and inappropriate content should be reported.**
- **Don't post anything that would embarrass you later.**
- **Don't mislead people into thinking that you're older or younger.**

(www.myspace.com/Modules/Common/Pages/SafetyTips.aspx)

Internet Wisdom

Meeting different people is part of the charm and fun of the Internet. Experts say chatting is okay. But everyone should learn the danger signals. Experts have some tips about how to spot a predator. Predators may try to give young people gifts or money. They may ask for photos. They may talk about sex. They may tell a young friend to lie to his or her parents or keep the friendship secret. They may ask for a private meeting.

Experts also say that teens should listen to their gut feelings. If something feels weird, it probably is. If a teen thinks Internet friends are lying about their age, they probably are. Teens who listen to their gut feelings have more chance of staying safe.

Taking Control

Internet predators can be scary. But smart users protect themselves. They know safe ways to explore the Internet. Kids are used to adults telling them what to do. But few young people are used to adults who try to con them. That is why understanding predators is so important. Young people themselves can poison the Internet for predators. They can do this by refusing to play their games.

Notes

Chapter 1: Cyber-Creeps

1. Quoted in Nigel Bunyan, "Internet Exchanges That Expose Studabaker's Lies," Telegraph.co.uk, February 13, 2004. www.telegraph.co.uk/news/main.jhtml?xml=/news/2004/02/13/wstud313.xml.
2. Quoted in Mark Mueller, "To Catch a Monster, Using Anti-Terror Law," *Pittsburgh Star Ledger*, August 14, 2005. www.nj.com/news/ledger/index.ssf?/news/ledger/stories/patriotact/partfour.html.
3. Quoted in Mueller, "To Catch a Monster, Using Anti-Terror Law."
4. Quoted in Mark Wineka, "Cooper, Law Enforcement Warn Parents About Sexual Predators," *Salisbury (NC) Post*, August 18, 2006. www.salisburypost.com/index.php.

Chapter 2: Survivors

5. Quoted in Katherine Tarbox, *A Girl's Life Online*. New York: Plume, 2001, p. 49.
6. Tarbox, *A Girl's Life Online*, p. 152.
7. Tarbox, *A Girl's Life Online*, p. 164.
8. Tarbox, *A Girl's Life Online*, p. 187.

9. Quoted in "House Committee on Energy and Commerce, Hearing on Sexual Exploitation of Children Over the Internet: What Parents, Kids, and Congress Need to Know About Sexual Predators," April 4, 2006. http://energy commerce.house.gov/108/Hearings/0404 2006hearing1820/Berry.pdf#search=%22%2 2justin%20berry%22%20testimony%20con gress%22.

10. Quoted in Kurt Eichenwald, "Through His Webcam, a Boy Joins the Sordid Online World," *New York Times,* December 19, 2005. www.nytimes.com/2005/12/19/national/19 kids.ready.html?ei=5090&en=aea51b3919b2 361a&ex=1292648400.

11. Quoted in House Committee on Energy and Commerce.

12. Quoted in Eichenwald, "Through his Web cam, a Boy Joins the Sordid Online World."

Chapter 3: Catching Predators

13. Mark Vasto, "Inside the Sick World of Internet Predators," *Parkville Luminary* On-line, August 18, 2006. http://parkvilleluminary. com/news/platte_county/inside_the_sick_ world_of_internet_predators.php.

14. Quoted in Vasto, "Inside the Sick World of Internet Predators."

15. Quoted in Lori Stuenkel, "Trolling for Sex Offenders," *Gilroy Dispatch,* May 5, 2005.

www.gilroydispatch.com/news/contentview.asp
?c=157815.

16. Del Harvey, "PeeJ Profile: Del Harvey,"
Perverted-Justice.com. www.perverted-justice.
com/?pg=profiledel.

17. Quoted in Chris Hansen, "To Catch a Predator III." transcript, MSNBC.com. http://
msnbc.msn.com/id/11152602/.

18. Quoted in Hansen, "To Catch a Predator III."

Chapter 4: Staying Safe

19. Quoted in Pamela Tom, "Kids Learn How to
Spot Online Predators," transcript, KGO-TV
ABC 7, December 15, 2005. http://abclocal.
go.com/kgo/story?section=assignment_7&id=
3729962.

20. Sarah Wright, "Discussion: MySpace and
Deleting Online Predators Act (DOPA),"
MIT News Office. www.danah.org/papers/
MySpaceDOPA.pdf#search=%22%22discus
sion%3A%20myspace%20and%20deleting
%20online%20predators%20act%20(dopa)
%22.

21. Wereon2u.ca, "Homepage," www.weron2u.
ca/home.

22. Weron2u.ca, "What You Can Do," www.wer
on2u.ca/home.

23. Quoted in Tom, "Kids Learn How to Spot
Online Predators."

Glossary

cybersex: Sex activity done with talk or pictures over the computer.

decoys: People who play a role to lure or fool another person.

grooming: Making friends with a child or teen just to get him or her ready for sex.

pedophile: A person who is turned on by sex with children.

pornography: Pictures or writing about sex, also called porn. Porn that shows children or teens is against the law in the United States.

predators: People who have committed an illegal sex offense. People who hunt for or hurt others, especially sexually.

solicitation: A sex advance or invitation.

sting: A setup by police and others to catch a person who is committing a crime.

Bibliography

Books

John R. Levine, Margaret Levine Young, and Carol Baroudi, *The Internet for Dummies*. Hoboken, NJ: Wiley, 2005. This book is for everyone who wants to surf the Web. It has many hints about online safety.

Katherine Tarbox, *A Girl's Life Online*. New York: Plume, 2004. This is the true story of a young girl who was taken in by an Internet predator. She tells what happened to her and how she got over it.

Web Sites

i-SAFE (www.isafe.org). This is a large site. It says it is the leader in Internet safety education. The area for teens has tips for cyber-safety in the virtual training academy. Teens may also share experiences with others at the i-SAFE blog.

Julia Layton, "How MySpace Works," How StuffWorks (http://computer.howstuffworks.

com/myspace.htm). This series of articles by an Internet expert tells how MySpace works. It explains what people do on MySpace. There is a lot about safety, too.

LiveWires Design (www.livewwwires.com). At this site, people can explore the Missing game. There are several links that tell why and how it was created.

SafeTeens.com (www.safeteens.com). This site gives teens lots of safety tips for exploring online.

Weron2u.ca (www.weron2u.ca/home). Visitors to this site learn about predator tactics. They can read true stories and learn how to be safe on the Internet.

"What's New?" Information for Young Adults, NetSafe (www.netsafe.org.nz/youngadults/youngadults_default.aspx). There are links on this site to learn all about grooming. Teens can learn how to recognize grooming and how to protect themselves from groomers.

Wired Kids.org (www.wiredkids.org/index.html). Kids, tweens, and teens can learn how to report predators. At the site for teens, there is an online community with classes, clubs, and many teen activities. There are plenty of tips about safety in cyberspace.

Index

Abbey (decoy), 34–35
Al (predator), 20

Bell, Jason, 36–38
Berry, Justin, 28–31
Bianco, Chad, 43
Boyd, Danah, 49–50

Catrina (decoy), 36–38
chat rooms, 8
child porn, 11, 15, 29–30
children. *See* young people
Crimes Against Children
  Research Center, 45
cybersex, 29–30

Dateline (television series),
  5, 38–43
Davis, Bobbi, 20
decoys, 32, 34–38
Dos Reis, Saul, 28

force
  murder, 26, 28
  used by predators, 10,
    17–18, 20

games, 53–54
grooming, 9–10, 13–14

Hansen, Chris, 40, 43
Harvey, Del, 38–40, 42
Herald Community
  Newspapers, 17

Internet
  blocking sites, 49–50
  number of young people
    using, 4
  policing by sites, 45,
    47–48
  safety education sites,
    51–53
i-SAFE, 51
Italia, Cris, 17

Jackson, David, 34–35

Kufrovich, Frank, 23–25
Kozakiewicz, Alicia,
  16–18, 19

laws, 45–46
LiveWires Design, 53–54
Long, Christina, 26, 28
love, as bait, 9, 14

Madruga, Mitch, 36–38
Mark (predator), 22–25
Mercer, Kim, 46
Missing (game), 53–54
Morrel, Julian, 13–15
murder, 26, 28
MySpace
  policing by, 47
  popularity of, 50
  used by predators, 28, 29

NeoPets.com, 7

New York Times (newspaper), 31

O'Connell, Wendy, 37

pedophiles, 7, 17
see also predators
Perverted-Justice.com (PeeJ)
Dateline and, 38–42
police and, 35–38, 39
predators
age of, 10, 13, 29
characteristics of, 7, 17, 43
force used by, 10, 17–18, 20
secret lives of, 12, 18
tactics, 9–10, 13–14, 53–54
Pre-Teen chat, 13
prison, 45–46

safety
games about, 53–54
knowing about, 50
sites with information about, 52–53
tips, 54
Scott (pedophile), 17
sex
legal age in states, 32
trust and, 9–10, 13
use of force and, 10, 17–18, 20
sex slaves, 17
social sites
policing by, 45, 47–48
young people and, 50

solicitations, 7–9
stings
Dateline, 38–43
police, 32, 34–38
Studabaker, Toby, 7, 9–12

Tarbox, Katie, 21–25
teenagers. *See* young people
TeenSpot, 48
"To Catch a Predator" (television show), 5, 38–43
trust, sex and, 9–10, 13
Tyree, Scott, 16–18, 19

Vasto, Mark, 34
victims
characteristics of, 19–20
emotions of, 20, 24–25, 30–31
grooming of, 9–10, 13–14
violence
murder, 26, 28
used by predators, 10, 17–18, 20

Weron2u, 52–53
Whitley, Steve, 18

Xanga, 50

young people
number solicited, 7–9, 45
number using Internet, 4
as predators, 29
predators pretending to be, 10, 13
social sites and, 50

Picture Credits

Cover: AP/Wide World Photos

About the Author

Toney Allman has degrees from Ohio State University and University of Hawaii. She lives in Virginia where she enjoys writing nonfiction books for students.